A Special Bravery

A Special Bravery

By JOHANNA JOHNSTON

ILLUSTRATED BY ANN GRIFALCONI

Dodd, Mead & Company · New York

For Bessie Barnes Madden,
a long-time friend

Contents

A Special Bravery

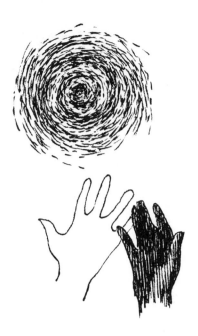

Christopher Columbus sailed
across the ocean and found
a new land, America.
El Negro, a dark man,
steered one of his ships.

After Columbus, came
soldiers and explorers
and some of these
were black men too.

White men and women and black men and women
lived and worked in Jamestown colony
before ever the Pilgrims landed
on Plymouth Rock.

White men and dark men
were settling America together...
And then something happened.

11

It happened because men found they needed
many hard-working helpers to clear and farm
the wild, new land.
And no matter how they tried
they could not get enough workers
to come from Europe.
At last it seemed to some men
that the only answer
was the old, old, bad one
of slavery.

Men had already found that
in Africa
they could capture
men and women and children.
They were taking those captured people
to be slaves in the West Indies.
Now they began capturing Negroes
and bringing them to America.
Hundreds, then thousands, of Negroes
were brought from Africa to America
and put to work.

Some of the Negroes who were brought
to America
became free.
But not many.
Most Negroes were not allowed
to do anything or be anybody
except what their masters said
they could do or be.
That was slavery.

So it was not easy for Negroes
to show the kind of
proud and talented people they were.
It took a very SPECIAL bravery.

The people in this book
are just a few of the Negroes
who had
that kind of bravery.

Crispus Attucks

Crispus Attucks was a sailing man.
He sailed on a whaling ship out of Boston
long ago.
One day his ship sailed back into Boston harbor
after a long voyage, and when
Crispus Attucks got off his ship he could see that
there was trouble in Boston.
English soldiers in red coats marched up and down
the waterfront.
Here and there, men stood in little groups and
watched the soldiers with frowning faces.
Crispus Attucks found some men he knew.
He asked them what was wrong.
"Wrong?" said one of the men. "You *have* been away,
not to know. The King of England has gone too far,
that's what. First he sent word
that we must pay taxes that we never
paid before. We let him know we had a right to vote
on such matters. And what did he do?

He sent soldiers to *make* us pay."
The man shook his fist at the soldiers.
Another man said, "It looks like the king has forgotten
we are Americans. He's trying to order us around
like slaves."

Crispus Attucks was quiet for a moment.
He was a tall, strong, dark man—a Negro.
He knew very well what it was to be a slave.
He had been a slave, owned by a man who
lived a long way from Boston.
But as soon as he was grown,
Crispus Attucks had run away.
He had come to Boston and signed on a ship
as a sailor. He had been happy after that.
But now he was troubled as he heard
what the men were saying.
"The king is trying to make slaves of us all,"
said one. Another said, "If only
we could get rid of those soldiers.
They march up and down as if
they owned us all."
Suddenly Crispus Attucks spoke.

"Nobody wants to be a slave," he said.
"And the way to get rid of the soldiers is
to march right at them and send them running."
The other men looked at him.
What he said sounded good to them.
"That's right," said one. And he picked up a stick.
"Come on, let's go," said another,
picking up a stone. All the men agreed,
and picked up sticks and stones. Then
they began to march toward the soldiers.
Crispus Attucks, tall and strong and dark,
marched with them.
"Go away," the men called to the soldiers.
"Go back to England where you belong.
We're all free Americans here."
The soldiers were frightened as the men
came nearer and nearer.
They raised their guns and began firing.
"Stop!" cried their captain.
"Those men have done nothing to hurt you."
But before the soldiers heard their captain
they had shot five Americans.
The first to fall was Crispus Attucks.

16

The men of Boston set up a monument to
Crispus Attucks, a Negro who had been a slave.
They honored him as Americans always will.
He was the first American to die
in the war against England that made
America free.

James Forten

"All right," said the captain of the ship.
"You want to go to sea with me and
fight the English.
Would you like to be a powder boy?"
James Forten asked, "What is a powder boy?"
"You'll see," said the captain.
"Would I really be helping to win the war?" asked James.
He was just a boy, not yet fourteen,
and lively and dark and quick.
The captain said, "Yes, you would really be helping."
"Then I'll do it," said James.
He ran home to say goodbye to his family.
He got a little bundle of clothes.
Then he ran back to get aboard the ship.
Soon it sailed out of the harbor at
Philadelphia and out to sea.
James learned that his job was to help
look after the gunpowder
that was used to fire the cannon on the ship.

19

He had to do more.
When the American sailors saw an English ship,
they sailed closer to it to fight.
Then James Forten, the powder boy,
had to make sure that the sailors at the cannon
had gunpowder when they needed it.
The first sea fight went well
for the Americans.
They defeated the English and
took some English prisoners.
They sailed on and
fought again and won.
But then came a battle
that the Americans did not win.
The English ship came alongside of
the American ship.
The English sailors came aboard the
American ship and began taking prisoners.
An English sailor grabbed James Forten,
the powder boy.

Then the sailor looked at him and
felt sorry. He said, "You are so young.
You are a Negro too. And Negroes do not have
a very happy time in America. Would you like to
come home to England with me and live there?"
It was a kind offer the Englishman was making.
But James Forten shook his head.
"Thank you," he said, "but I am an American
like everyone else aboard this ship.
We are all fighting for freedom together.
Whatever happens to the others must happen to me too."
So the English sailor had to take James Forten
prisoner, and young James
was a prisoner for a long time.

At last the war was over
and the Americans had won.
America did not belong to England any more
and Americans were free. James Forten
was free too.
He went home to Philadelphia and
he started a business,
making sails for ships.

22

He did very well and white men and black
both respected him.
But that was really no surprise.
He had showed what sort of man he would be
when he was just a boy,
proudly refusing to be anything
but an American.

Benjamin Banneker

Tick, tock. The clock worked.
Ding! Ding! When the hands marked the hour
it chimed.
Benjamin Banneker had made the clock
all by himself.
"That is a wonderful clock," said a man
who lived near the Banneker farm.
"I really think that it is the first chiming clock

25

that anyone has ever made in America. How
did you learn to make it?"

What could young Benjamin Banneker say?
He had not learned how to make it
from anyone.
He had figured it out for himself,
looking at how clocks worked,
thinking about what kinds of gears and wheels
were needed. Then he had made
the gears and wheels for himself.
And after that, he had fitted them together,
first this way, then that way—
over and over—until at last,
they moved back and forth as they should.
Tick, tock, tick, tock, DING!

"You are a remarkable young man,"
said the neighbor.
"Have you gone to school at all?"
Yes, Benjamin had been lucky.
His father was not a slave, but a free man,
and owned his own little farm in Maryland.

There had been a school nearby where
Negro children could go.
Benjamin had learned to read and write.
But then he had read all the books in the school.
He could not find any more books to read
anywhere.
He wanted to study. He wanted to learn more.
But he couldn't.
So he worked on his father's farm.
But even though he had to work hard
with his hands, he would not give up and
stop using his mind.
He figured out ways to improve the farm tools.
He figured out ways to do many things
better than they had been done before.
Then he went to work on the clock and
made it work!
"A young man like you deserves help,"
said the neighbor. "What can I do to help you?"
"Could you lend me books to read?" asked
Benjamin Banneker.
The neighbor could lend him books
and did.

They were hard books about mathematics,
and surveying land, and astronomy.
But Benjamin Banneker read them all and
learned everything in them. He learned
how to do the hardest problems.
He learned about the stars and the heavens.
And he learned how to survey land.
The neighbor was so impressed by what
Benjamin Banneker had learned that
he talked to Thomas Jefferson, the man who
had written the Declaration of Independence.
The war was over by this time and
Jefferson and George Washington and many others
were working to build a new nation of
the United States.
Thomas Jefferson thought of how the
brilliant Negro, Benjamin Banneker,
could help.
Then Jefferson asked Banneker to join the men
who were surveying land for the new capital city of
Washington, D.C.
So Benjamin Banneker traveled to Washington and
helped to lay out and plan that city.

Today when we visit Washington, D.C.
we can remember a Negro boy who would not give up—
who made a clock when he had no books to read—
Benjamin Banneker.

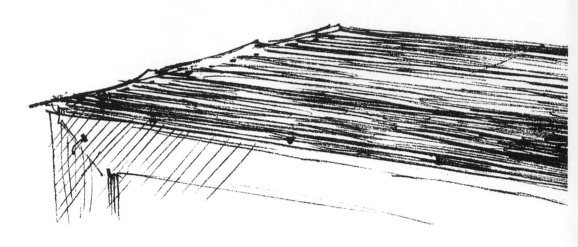

Henry Brown

Bang! Bang! Bang! The hammer
pounded in the nails
and at last the big wooden box
was all closed up. And inside the box
was a very happy man.
How could he be happy, nailed up in a box?
But he was.
His name was Henry Brown and he lived
in the South, where the laws about slavery
were harder than anywhere else.
He was a slave and his wife and his children

were slaves. And just a little while before,
the white man who owned him and his family had
sold Henry Brown's wife and children to a man
who lived far away.
Henry Brown had been in despair.
Then he had a daring plan.
He talked about it secretly
with a white man who was his friend.
The friend agreed to help him.
The friend was following the plan when
he nailed Henry Brown into the box.

31

When the box was nailed up tight,
the friend called a helper and
together they lifted the box onto a wagon.
The wagon rattled off to the station.
At the station, more men lifted the box
off the wagon. They did not know
what was in it.
It was just a box to bump and bang aboard
the freight car when the train came in.
Inside the box, Henry Brown was cramped and
hungry and thirsty. The box jolted with
every jolt of the train.
But Henry Brown was still happy.
If no one found out that he was in the box
his wonderful plan would work.

The train stopped.
More men moved the box.
They bumped and banged it
into the hold of a ship.
Henry Brown lost track of time.
He did not know if it was night or day
in his box. The box pitched back and forth

with the roll of the ship and
Henry Brown had just one thought.
He must not cry out or someone
might find out he was in the box,
and then his plan would fail.

At last, the trip on the water was over.
There were more bumpings and bangings.
There was another wagon ride.
Then the box was set down.
Someone began to pull out the nails
to open the box.
Henry Brown held his breath.
Was it a friend?
The last boards were pulled loose.
"Come out, Henry Brown," said someone.
He was the man to whom
Henry Brown's friend in the South had
addressed the box.
Henry Brown blinked. It was hard to move.
Finally, he got out and stood up.
The friendly man before him was smiling.
Henry Brown had done it. He had escaped from the South

and slavery. He was in the North, where
Negroes were not slaves.
Now he could work and find a way to get
his wife and children from the South also.
They would all be free and
Henry Brown could work with the men and women
who were trying to have slavery ended everywhere.

Many people began to call him "Box" Brown after
they heard his story.
But the nickname was a kind one and
it helped to remind everyone of what a bad thing
slavery could be—so bad
that a brave man had to be shipped in a box
to escape it.

Harriet Tubman

The woods were dark all around her.
There was no road, no path,
no trail.
She could only tell what direction she was going
by looking up at the stars and following the
bright one that hung low
in the north.
When clouds covered the sky so that it was dark too,
she had to feel her way. She
put out her hands and felt the tree trunks.
Moss grew on the northern side of tree trunks.
She felt for the moss and where it grew it
showed her the way.

When day came, she had to hide
in bushes or behind rocks. When there were storms
she had nothing but bushes or trees
to cover her.
After a while, she had no more food.

Sometimes she found berries. And she drank
from brooks.

On and on she went, night after night,
covering mile after mile.

Sometimes, not often, she came near a house
where she thought there were people who
would help her.

She would go to the house when it was dark,
and the people would hide her for a day
while she ate something and rested.

Then when night came, she would
start on again.

At last, after many nights and days,
Harriet Tubman knew she was out of the South,
where she had been a slave.
She was in the North where Negroes could be free.
Soon she was in the city of Philadelphia

where there were white men and women who
would help her.

She made her way to those people and
they welcomed her with joy.

Harriet Tubman was safe and free.

"Now you must rest," they told her.

"After that, we will find you a place to live
and a job so that you can have a good life."

Harriet said, "Thank you. Yes, I want a job
for a while. But as soon as I have earned
a little money, I must go back down South again."

"Go South again?" said her friends.

They were horrified.

"How can you think of making that terrible journey again?"

Harriet said, "I have brothers there, and
my mother and father. I have friends—all of them
still in slavery. Now that I know the way
I must go back and lead them to freedom also."

Her friends said, "You can't bring so many.
You will be caught."

Harriet said, "I will just have to make many trips."

Nobody could make her change her mind.

Before many weeks had passed, she was on her way.

She had to travel to the South as secretly
as she had left it.
She had to be very secret as she
got in touch with her family and friends.
They decided who would make the first trip
back with her.
Then there was the trip north again,
in the dark, following the star.
But this time it was even more dangerous,
for there were more people.
Harriet made everyone move as quietly as a
shadow.
At last all of them were safely in the North,
in freedom.

Again Harriet Tubman rested and then worked awhile.
Then she went back to the South to
bring more slaves to freedom.
Before the war came that ended slavery,
Harriet Tubman had made nineteen journeys.
She had faced all sorts of dangers, but
she had brought more than three hundred men and women
from slavery to freedom.

39

Frederick Douglass

There was a room full of people around him—
two hundred people or more. They were all
looking at him.
The man beside him said, "Go on. Get up.
Talk. They want to hear about all
that you have done."

Frederick Douglass had done many
hard things in his life.
This seemed the hardest of all.
But he did it. He got up.
He looked at all the people. He tried to speak,
but his voice made no sound.
He tried again. This time
he did better. He began to tell
the people in the room about his life.
He told them how he had been born a slave
in Maryland.

He had hardly seen his mother because she was
a slave who had to work in the fields.
He told of a kind woman who had taught him
to read and write.
But then his life had grown harder.
His master had whipped him again and again.
He told of how he had tried to run away.
But almost at once he had been caught
and whipped again.
He told of how he had tried a second time
to run away to the North.
This time he had done it.
He was in the North now. He had
married the girl he loved.
He had a job.
Then he told the room full of people that
he was doing something very dangerous right now.
Just speaking out as he was could mean that
his owner, in the South, would hear where he was
and then send slave-catchers to
find him and take him back to the South.
But he was glad to tell the story anyway.
It might help people in the North to

realize what slavery was like.
Frederick Douglass finished speaking and
sat down. And everybody in the room
clapped and cheered—and cried a little too.
They had never heard anyone tell them so plainly
about slavery before.
Then they came to shake Frederick Douglass' hand
and to tell him that they were going to work
harder than ever for a law that would
end slavery in America.

After that first speech that was
so hard to make,
Frederick Douglass made more and more speeches.
He became famous all over the North as
one of the country's greatest speakers.
And he made
thousands of people realize
that slavery must be ended.
He wrote a book about his life
and many people read it.
He put out a magazine for people who
were working to end slavery.

At last a war came between the North
and the South, mostly because of slavery.
President Lincoln invited Frederick Douglass
to the White House. He asked him to help
recruit Negroes as soldiers.
After the war, when slavery was ended,
Frederick Douglass had many important
government jobs.
And for all of his long, busy life, he was a man
who spoke out clearly and well
for freedom for *all* Americans.

Robert Smalls

It was night and so dark
that a person could hardly see
the ships at anchor in the harbor.
They were warships—gunboats and cruisers and
even bigger warships. And they belonged
to the South.
The states of the South and the North
were at war.
They were fighting each other because the North
did not want any more slavery
in the United States and the South did.

Outside the dark harbor where the
Southern warships lay,
out in the sea beyond,
there were Northern warships,
sailing back and forth,
to make sure that the Southern ships
did not come out of the harbor.

45

Down to the dark harbor came a man.

His name was Robert Smalls.

He was a sailor on one of the Southern warships.

But he did not want to fight for the South.

He was a Negro and a slave, and he was helping
the Southern cause only
because he had to.

But now he had a plan.

He waited in the dark very quietly.

Soon more shadows came out of the dark
and stood near him.

His brother was there. And his wife
and his children.

"Shhh," said Robert Smalls.

Then he helped his wife and his children
and his brother get into a little rowboat.

Very quietly,
Robert Smalls rowed the boat
out to the gunboat on which he served
every day.

Robert Smalls helped his wife and children
and his brother get on board the gunboat.
Then everyone sat quietly
in the dark . . . except for Robert Smalls.
He went down below and
got the engines going.
Then he came on deck and put on
the captain's hat and coat.
The engines were working quietly.
Robert Smalls pulled the captain's hat
down over his ears and went to the wheel
and started the gunboat out of the harbor.
Chuff! Chuff! Chuff!
The gunboat sailed by the other Southern ships.
Robert Smalls gave the right signal
to each ship.
Chuff! Chuff! Chuff!
Robert Smalls sailed the gunboat on —
out into the open sea.
The dawn was coming.
Robert Smalls and his family saw
other ships on the horizon.
They were the Northern warships.

Robert Smalls steered the gunboat right up to
the biggest Northern ship.
The captain came to the rail of the Northern ship.
"Who are you?" he asked.
"What are you doing here?"
"I am Robert Smalls," said the dark man
on the Southern gunboat.
"I have brought this Southern ship to you
so that it may fight for the North instead of
the South. I want to fight for the North too."

Robert Smalls and his family
were welcomed in the North.
Robert Smalls was given a prize for
bringing a Southern warship to the North
and everyone honored him
for doing such a brave deed.

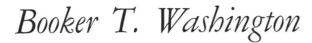

Booker T. Washington

Some boys and girls stood watching a
serious young man beside a big pile of wet clay.
The young man had clay all over him, but he was not
paying any attention to that. He was trying to
shape the clay into bricks and then
stack the bricks in a pile.
"Come on," said the young man to the boys and girls.
"You're supposed to be doing this too."
One boy spoke. "But we don't know how to make bricks."
The young man said, "I don't know how to make them
very well either. We'll learn as we do it."
One of the girls said, "I didn't come to school
to learn to make BRICKS."
The young man looked at the girl, and then at
all of the girls and boys. Then he spoke,
very seriously. "We won't even have a school if
we don't learn to make bricks," he said.

The war between the North and South was over.

Slavery had ended. No Negroes anywhere in America
were slaves any more.
They were free.
But most of them were very poor.
And in all the states where slavery had been,
very few Negroes knew how to read and write.
Without reading and writing, they could not get jobs
to earn money.
They needed schools more than anything else,
and there weren't many schools for them.

The young man, whose name was
Booker T. Washington,
had worked very hard to go to school himself.
He had walked hundreds of miles from his home
to find a school that would teach him
all that he wanted to know.
When he finished school his one dream was to
help start more schools for poor boys and girls.
Now he was in Alabama where some people had promised
to help him start a school.
They gave him an old, falling-down building for it.
The building had to be fixed and bricks were needed.

"Come on," said Booker T. Washington to the
boys and girls around him. "In your hearts
you want a school. With your hands you can help to
build it. Then you can work with your heads as well.
It is always best to work with all three—
your heart, your hands, your head."
The boys and girls all picked up handfuls of clay.
They began trying to make bricks.
They did not have an easy time.
After the bricks were shaped they had to be
dried and baked. The boys and girls did not know
how to bake them. Neither did Booker T. Washington.
But they kept on trying,
again and again,
until at last they had made the bricks.

They made many things that they had never made before
with Booker T. Washington helping them and
working as hard as they did.
Finally, they made a school where they could live and study.
Every day as they worked they had lessons too.
They worked with their heads as well as their hands.
The school grew and grew.

More and more poor boys and girls came to it
and learned how to study and how to work.
They left the school ready to be
useful, happy men and women.
Booker T. Washington's school—
Tuskegee Institute in Alabama—
became famous all over America.
It was almost as famous as Booker T. Washington himself,
the man who would not be stopped by
not having any bricks,
a man who would make bricks himself and learn
and teach
while he did it.

George Washington Carver

Peanuts—peanuts—what are peanuts good for?
The farmer did not think they were good for much.
Pigs could dig them up and eat them.
People could roast them and eat them now and then.
That was all.
The young teacher from Booker T. Washington's school
did not know what else peanuts were good for either.
But he wished that he could think of SOMETHING.
Peanuts grew like weeds on the land in Alabama.

The young teacher found an empty room
at the school.
He got a little stove and some jars and bottles
and other things scientists use. And he got
lots and lots of peanuts.
Then he went to work.
He boiled some peanuts and he froze some.
He smashed some and he squeezed some and
he dried some.

Day after day, week after week, month after month,
he was always doing something
with peanuts.
The other teachers could not think what he
was up to.
It seemed foolish to them for anyone
to spend so much time with
peanuts.
The young teacher did not let what
people said stop him.
He kept on with what he was doing.
Then, one day, he was ready
to show some friends what that was.
He asked them to come to his room.
Then he showed them
bottles of oil—made from peanuts,
cans of flour—made from peanuts,
jars of delicious butter—made from peanuts.
He showed them cheese, candy, coffee, soap—
almost three hundred different products—
all made from peanuts.
His friends were astonished.

They thought the young teacher must be
a magician.
And he was—
where plants were concerned.

His name was George Washington Carver,
and he had done a wonderful thing for
the farmers of Alabama.
Now they could give their lands a rest from
growing cotton.
They could grow peanuts on the land and
make money from them.
George Washington Carver went on to see
how many things he could make from
sweet potatoes.
He made flour, starch, meal,
paste, ink,
molasses,
and dozens of other things—
from sweet potatoes.
He became so well known for the magical uses
he could find for growing things that
the famous inventor, Thomas Alva Edison,

asked if he would come north and work with him.
George Washington Carver was grateful but
he preferred to stay in the South at Tuskegee.
President Roosevelt came to visit Tuskegee
one day. Whom did he especially ask to see?
George Washington Carver.
All the world honors him for what he did,
but boys and girls can thank him
most of all for
peanut butter.

Matthew Henson

Snow and ice were everywhere,
as far as the eye could see.
No men had ever been there before,
but now there were six men,
looking tiny in the wilderness of snow and ice—
six men, some sleds and some sled dogs.

It was so cold that the men's fur hoods
froze to their cheeks.
The ice on which they were traveling
was not smooth. It was rough and jagged.
They had to use picks to hack out a trail.
On and on, they struggled,
farther and farther from the ship which had
brought them to the edge of this land of ice.
They were trying to reach
the top of the world,
the North Pole,
where no man had been before.

Who were the men trying to do this brave
and difficult thing?
One was a white man, Commander Peary.
One was a Negro, Matthew Henson, his friend and helper.
And four were Eskimo guides.
Day by day they drew nearer to their goal.
Then they came to a thin spot of ice.
One sled fell through the ice.
Matthew Henson was steering the sled.
He fell into the icy water too.
It was so cold he could have become a block of ice
in an instant.
But an Eskimo grabbed Matthew Henson and
pulled him out of the freezing water.
Matthew Henson thanked the Eskimo and so
did Commander Peary.
Matthew Henson had traveled with the Commander for years,
in hot countries as well as this cold one.
The Commander did not think he could go on if
Matthew Henson was not beside him,
driving the dogs, telling the Eskimos what to do,
scouting the trail, helping in some way
every minute of the day.

61

Now, with Matthew Henson beside him again,
the Commander traveled on,
another day and another.
Then, on the next day, the Commander stopped and
looked at his charts and his instruments.
Then he drove a stick into the ice and
put an American flag on the stick.

He called Matthew Henson to stand beside him.
They were standing at the North Pole.
Two Americans—one white and one black—
had made the fearful, wonderful journey
to that spot
together.

63

When Commander Peary and Matthew Henson
came back to the United States
they were given many honors for having been
the first men to reach the North Pole.
Commander Peary wrote a book about it and
so did Matthew Henson.

They did not do any more exploring.
Exploring is for young men.
But all his life Matthew Henson remembered
the excitement of going to
far, unknown places.
All his life he remembered the thrill he had felt
when he and Commander Peary
stood together at the top of the world,
the first men to stand there.

Mary McLeod Bethune

"We'll make pies," said Mary McLeod Bethune.
"We'll make sweet potato pies and sell them and
get enough money for pencils and books."
It was a long time since Booker T. Washington
had built his school at Tuskegee, but
there were still very few schools for Negroes
in the South. There were no schools for Negro girls
in Florida at all.
Mary McLeod Bethune had made up her mind to start a
school for girls in Daytona, Florida.
She had one dollar and a half. But
Mrs. Bethune did not let that worry her.
She had five little girls for her first students,
and that was a start.
With them beside her, she rented a dirty, tumble-down
cabin, and promised to pay the rent later.
A friend lent them an old cookstove and some pie pans.
A farmer sold them some sweet potatoes and eggs
on credit.

Then Mary McLeod Bethune and the five little girls
began to make sweet potato pies.
They all worked together with big aprons tied
around their waists.
They peeled potatoes and boiled them and
they beat eggs,
and while they worked, Mary McLeod Bethune
gave them a geography lesson.
The girls hardly knew it was a lesson, because
they were having such fun.
Then, when the pies were baking and the lesson was over,
they sang together.

When the pies were baked, all golden brown,
Mary McLeod Bethune and the five little girls
put the pies in a wagon and covered them well.
They pulled the wagon down the road to
where a lot of men were building a railroad.
The men were happy to buy
nice, fresh sweet potato pies.
Mary McLeod Bethune got enough money for the pies to buy
some pencils and books, and more
sweet potatoes and eggs to
bake more pies.
Every day she and the girls made pies and sold them
and had lessons. And day by day,
the tumble-down cabin became more and more
like a real school.

But Mary McLeod Bethune had a dream of a big building
with classrooms and a bedroom for every girl.
She thought about it so much it began to seem
almost as real as if it were really built.
One day she met a rich white man and told him
about her school. She even told him about the big building
with classrooms and bedrooms.

The next day the rich man came to visit her school.
He looked at the cabin. It was neat and tidy now,
but still a cabin.
He asked Mary McLeod where the big building was
that she had been talking about.
For a moment, Mrs. Bethune did not know what to say.
She realized that she had talked about a dream as though
it were real. Then she said,
"There is such a building—in my mind and
in my spirit. We will build it some day, I know."
The rich man was so impressed by
her faith that he said
he would give her money to help make her dream
come true. He said he would ask
some of his rich friends to help also.
And so, before very long, the big building
WAS real. Mrs. Bethune's school had more and more girls
as students, all learning to be
useful, intelligent women.

But as fast as the school grew, Mrs. Bethune
had more plans to help poor Negroes in the South.
She did so many things to help them and became

69

so well known that the President gave her
a high position in Washington, D.C., so that
she could help Negro young people
all over the country.

In her mind—in her spirit, Mary McLeod Bethune
saw a happier America where white people and Negroes
both had the same opportunities.
And she did all that she could,
all her life long,
to make that happier America come true.

Jackie Robinson

Twenty-five thousand people watched as
the dark, good-looking young man in a baseball uniform
stepped up to the plate and swung his bat.
He grounded out and
everyone sighed. Perhaps he was not going to be
any good after all.
Then he came up to bat a second time and
hit a home run!
The twenty-five thousand people cheered and
whistled and yelled with delight.
He made three more hits in that game
and stole a couple of bases as well.
After that, everybody was sure that it was
going to be all right.
Jackie Robinson, the first Negro to be asked to play
in big-league baseball, was going to be a success.
What was more, he was going to prove how wrong
the managers of big-league baseball had been
for years and years.

For years and years, Negro athletes had been showing
how good they were at all sorts of sports.
Joe Louis had won the world's boxing championship.
Jesse Owens had run faster than anybody else
in the world.
Negro baseball players on all-Negro teams were as good
as any white players.
But the managers of the big-league teams
never signed a Negro player.

It was all part of something that had started in
slavery days—something that made life hard for
every Negro in America.
It was a feeling that many white people had,
that the color of their skin made them better
than people whose skin was a darker color.
This ugly feeling—called prejudice—
made white people force dark people to live
different lives from their own.
In many places, white people kept dark people out of
their hospitals, their schools, their hotels—and
everywhere they kept them off their ball teams.

But fortunately, there were always
SOME white people who thought that way of behaving
was wrong.
The manager of the Dodgers baseball team was
such a person. He thought that it was time
that Negroes as well as whites should play on
big-league teams. The color of their skin didn't matter.
All that mattered was
how well they played ball.
The manager asked Jackie Robinson to be the first Negro
on the Dodgers team.
He chose him because he was a wonderful athlete.
He also chose him because he thought Jackie Robinson
was a calm, strong, young man who would not be upset
by all the things that might happen to him
because of being the first Negro in big-league baseball.
It took courage for Jackie Robinson to say yes,
he would play with the Dodgers.
He knew that there would be SOME white people
just waiting for him to fail.
But he also knew that if he did well he might be helping
to break down that ugly feeling of prejudice.

73

He said he would play with the Dodgers.
And he did better than anyone had dreamed he would.
The first year he played with the Dodgers
they won the pennant, and Jackie was named
Rookie of the Year.

Another year he was named
The Most Valuable Player in the National League.
When he finally quit playing baseball
he was elected to baseball's Hall of Fame.
He was proud of that, but even prouder
because more and more managers were asking Negroes
to play on their teams.
Now white and dark Americans alike
play and star
in America's favorite game.

Marian Anderson

When she was little she wanted a violin
more than anything else in the world.
Day after day, she saved the pennies she earned
by running errands or scrubbing the neighbors' steps,
and at last she was able to buy her very own violin.
It was just a cheap one and it squeaked a lot
but little Marian Anderson loved it
and played it until it fell to pieces.
By that time, she knew something else that
she wanted. And her sisters wanted it too.
A piano.
A piano cost a great deal more than a little,
squeaky violin. Marian could not hope to save enough
to buy a piano.
And then, one wonderful day, a piano was delivered
to the Anderson home in Philadelphia.
Marian's mother had managed to buy one.
Now Marian began playing the piano as once
she had played the violin.

Violins—pianos—the world had many instruments
that made beautiful music and
Marian loved them all.
She did not realize that she had
ONE instrument that could not be bought
that was as wonderful as any in the world—
her own voice.

Of course she sang. Her sisters sang too.
They sang at home. And they sang at church in the choir.
Marian just took that for granted.
But soon people who heard the sisters sing
began saying that Marian's voice was
special.
Marian began to realize that she liked to make music
by singing best of all.
And so, after she finished high school, she was
very happy when the members of her church
gave her money to take lessons from a
fine voice teacher.
Not long after that, when she was just seventeen,
she entered a big singing contest
and won.

Her voice WAS special.
Soon she was in New York, singing with
a great symphony orchestra.
Then she was in Europe, studying some more.
Then she was giving concerts in Europe,
and everyone was cheering the slim, dark young woman
from America.
When she was twenty-seven she gave
her first big concert in New York.
Everyone cheered her there also.
She had become a great singer, just as
the church members who had heard her
when she was little had said she would.
But the ugly feeling of prejudice which
some white Americans had for those who were darker
hurt Marian Anderson too.
Some white people did not want to let her sing
in their hall in Washington, D.C., because
she was a Negro.
Then the President's wife arranged for
Marian Anderson to sing on Easter Sunday
in front of the Lincoln Memorial.

Thousands of people heard her sing there and
were made happy by the beauty of her voice.
Thousands of people have heard her since then.
She has sung in New York's great Opera House.
She has sung all over America and
all over the world.

Violins,
pianos—
the world is full of musical instruments,
but it does not often hear a voice
like Marian Anderson's.

Ralph Bunche

Some angry men from Israel sat on one side
of a big table.
Some angry men from Egypt sat
on the other side.
They were quarreling because of some land they both wanted.
They were quarreling also because there was
a feeling of prejudice between
the men of Israel and the men of Egypt.
While they quarreled, other men all over the world
worried
and read their newspapers to find out
if they were coming any closer to
settling their quarrel.
If they did not settle it, men were afraid
that a new and terrible war would start.
Finally, the United Nations decided to send someone
to try to be a peacemaker.
The peacemaker came to the table
where the angry men were quarreling.

He was a pleasant, good-looking dark man and
he talked quietly.
He pointed out to the men from Israel that if
they gave up part of what they wanted they
might easily get something else in return.
He pointed out the same thing
to the men from Egypt.
Gradually, the angry men began to listen to him.

The men on one side of the table began to see
that the men on the other side were not really
so different from themselves.
At last, the man from the United Nations could smile
as he watched them sign
a treaty of peace with each other.
All the world felt better when it heard that
Ralph Bunche had settled the quarrel.

Ralph Bunche, the peacemaker, was a Negro from America.
Some Americans had been surprised
when the United Nations sent a Negro to help settle
such an important quarrel.
Perhaps they did not know that Ralph Bunche had studied
for many years in America's finest schools
and won many honors.
Perhaps they did not stop to think that just because
he was a Negro in America
Ralph Bunche had learned a lot about
that feeling called prejudice.
When he was a boy, going to school,
some schoolmates would not play with him,
just because he was a Negro.
When he went to high school, he could not be
on some teams, because of that.
Still, he had studied hard and done well.
And after college he worked for a long time
with a scientist
who was trying to find out
why
some people felt prejudice
toward others.

He helped the scientist write a book
to show Americans how they might destroy
their wonderful country if they did not get rid of
their feelings of prejudice.
The book became famous.

Yes, Ralph Bunche was a man who
knew very well how to talk with the angry men of
Israel and Egypt.
Because of the things that had been hard
in his own life,
he had learned how to help people feel
more friendly toward each other.

No wonder that when he came back to America
he was able to do more work for the United Nations.
No wonder that Ralph Bunche won the most famous
peace prize in the world—the Nobel Prize—
for helping to settle the Israel-Egypt quarrel.

Martin Luther King, Jr.

Sometimes it is brave to fight
for what one thinks is right,
as Crispus Attucks did.
Sometimes it takes even more bravery
NOT to fight, but just to do quietly
what one thinks is right.
Many Americans, both dark and white,
have proved that this is so
and one man who has helped them do it
is Martin Luther King, Jr.

A tired Negro woman had a seat on a bus.
A white woman got on the bus
and the driver told the Negro woman
to give up her seat
to the white woman.
The Negro woman said that there were other seats
on the bus where the white woman could sit. She
would not get up.

But this was in the South where
the feeling of prejudice against people with dark skins
stayed strong.
Police arrested the tired Negro woman who
would not stand up so the white woman could sit.
All of the Negroes of the city were angry
when they heard the news.
They met together and decided that
none of them would ride on buses
until the woman who had been arrested
was freed
and until there were new and fairer laws.
They wanted laws saying that
no Negro should have to stand in a bus
just because he was a Negro and that anybody,
white or dark, who got on a bus
that had empty seats
could have a seat.
Anybody, white or dark,
who got on a bus with no empty seats
should have to stand.
For all of one day no Negro in that city
rode on a bus.

That night a young Negro minister,
whose name was Martin Luther King, Jr.,
encouraged the people who had walked to work,
or to the store, or wherever they had to go.
He said that they should keep on walking
until the white people made fairer laws.

88

They should not be frightened or angry, but
just
keep
on
walking.
And that is what the Negroes of that city did.

Day after day, week after week, they walked
wherever they wanted to go.

Then many of the white people of the city
were angry at Martin Luther King.
Their bus lines were losing money.
Even worse, their consciences were beginning
to hurt.
In their hearts, they knew the Negroes
were right.
But they did not want to admit it.
They found a reason to arrest Martin Luther King.
Then someone threw a bomb at his house.
It did not hurt him or his wife or baby,
but it might have.
And all the Negroes of the city were very angry.
Some said the Negroes should all rise up
and throw bombs back at the white people.
But Martin Luther King stood on the porch of
his house, near the place where
the bomb had fallen,
and he said no.
Fighting would only make things worse.

90

He gave the people courage to just
go—on—walking—
until the white people made new laws.
So they walked and walked
for more than a year.
And at last all they hoped for came true.
The white people did make new laws.
White people and Negroes alike could sit in buses
when there were seats.
White people and Negroes alike had to stand
when the seats were filled.
Since then,
Martin Luther King has helped Negroes
in many parts of America,
showing them how they can
win their rights
by doing something braver than fighting.
They can refuse to be a part
of anything that is not fair to all.
He has helped white people
as well as black
to work together for a nation
where everyone is free.

Like Ralph Bunche, Martin Luther King won
the Nobel Peace Prize.
His life was ended
in a hard, cruel way.
But the world will always
remember and honor him.
And more and more
the world is beginning to see
and to honor
the very special bravery
of Negroes in America.

Other Facts about the People in This Book

CRISPUS ATTUCKS: born a slave about 1723, in Framingham, Massachusetts. Died March 5, 1770, in the Boston Massacre.

JAMES FORTEN: born 1766, in Philadelphia, Pennsylvania. Died 1842.

BENJAMIN BANNEKER: born 1731, in Maryland. Published a popular almanac, 1791-1802. Died 1806.

HENRY "BOX" BROWN: born a slave, 1816. Lectured for anti-slavery societies. Date of death uncertain.

HARRIET TUBMAN: born a slave about 1820, in Maryland. During the Civil War, she served the Union forces as a nurse and a spy. Died, 1913, in Auburn, New York.

FREDERICK DOUGLASS: born a slave, 1817, in Maryland. Held various political offices after the Civil War. Died 1895, in Washington, D.C.

ROBERT SMALLS: born a slave in 1839, in South Carolina. Served as Representative from South Carolina to the U.S. Congress for five terms after the Civil War. Died 1915.

BOOKER TALIAFERRO WASHINGTON: born a slave about 1856, in Virginia. Started Tuskegee Institute 1881. Died 1915.

GEORGE WASHINGTON CARVER: born about 1864 in Missouri. Became a teacher at Tuskegee Institute 1896. Died at Tuskegee 1943.

93

MATTHEW HENSON: born 1866. At North Pole with Commander Robert E. Peary April 6, 1909. Died 1955.

MARY MCLEOD BETHUNE: born 1875 in South Carolina. Founded what is now Bethune-Cookman College in Daytona, Florida, 1904. Worked with National Youth Administration and United Nations. Died 1955.

JACKIE ROBINSON: born in Georgia, 1919. Educated in California. Signed by the Dodgers in 1945, played first big-league baseball game in 1947.

MARIAN ANDERSON: born in Philadelphia 1908. Made her American debut in 1935. Sang with Metropolitan Opera in 1955. Gave a farewell concert in New York, 1965.

RALPH BUNCHE: born 1904 in Detroit, Michigan. Studied at University of California, Harvard, and London School of Economics. Was United Nations mediator between Israel and Egypt in 1948.

MARTIN LUTHER KING, JR.: born 1929 in Georgia. Helped lead bus boycott in Montgomery, Alabama, 1955. Killed by an assassin in Memphis, Tennessee, April 4, 1968.

The Author

Johanna Johnston's writing talent ranges from adult biographies to picture books for the very young. A particular interest in bringing to life great figures of the past and a broad knowledge of American history have led to her most recent titles—TOGETHER IN AMERICA, which weaves the story of the American Negro into the more familiar history of our country; THE CHALLENGE AND THE ANSWER, a book of famous American quotations set into their proper historical background; THOMAS JEFFERSON, HIS MANY TALENTS, which won a Thomas Alva Edison Award; adult books about Harriet Beecher Stowe and Victoria Woodhull.

For several years Miss Johnston wrote for radio, specializing in programs for children. Among her books for younger readers are EDIE CHANGES HER MIND, PENGUIN'S WAY, and the ever-popular SUGARPLUM.

Johanna Johnston was born and educated in Chicago, Illinois, and now lives and works in New York City. She is married and has one daughter.

The Artist

Ann Grifalconi is the author and illustrator of CITY RHYTHMS and has illustrated both adult and children's books, including THE JAZZ MAN, runner-up for the 1966 Newbery Award. A New Yorker by birth and by choice, she has been an art teacher in the New York City school system and is now a free-lance illustrator.